Dresses
COLORING BOOK!

Discover Amazing And Beautiful
Dresses Coloring Pages For Kids And Adults

COLORING BOOKS

This is a Bleed Through Page If You Are Using a Colouring Marker or Pen!
Find Other Great Titles By searching for Bold Illustrations on Your Favorite Book Retailer
Amazon.Ca | Barnes & Noble (BN.Com) | Books A Million (BAM.Com)

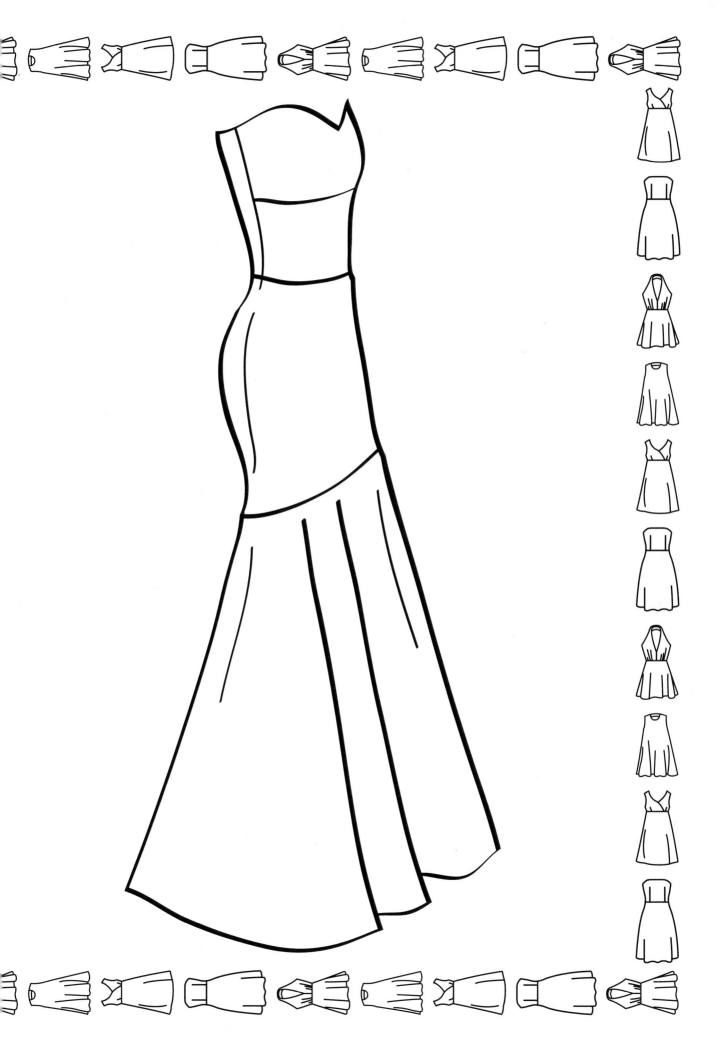

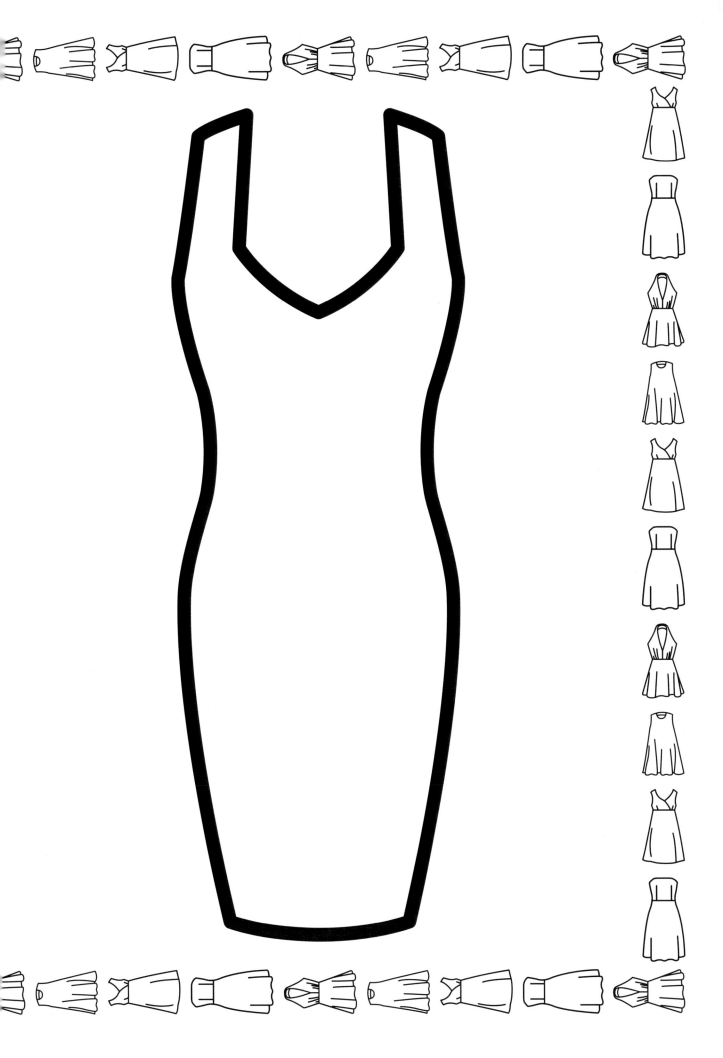

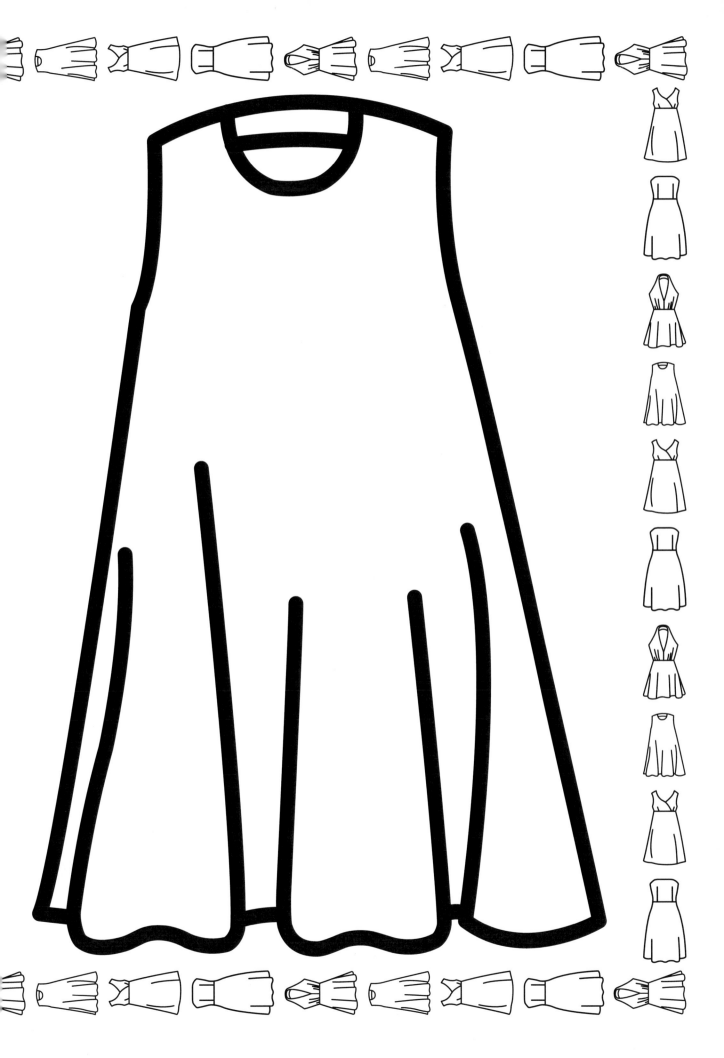

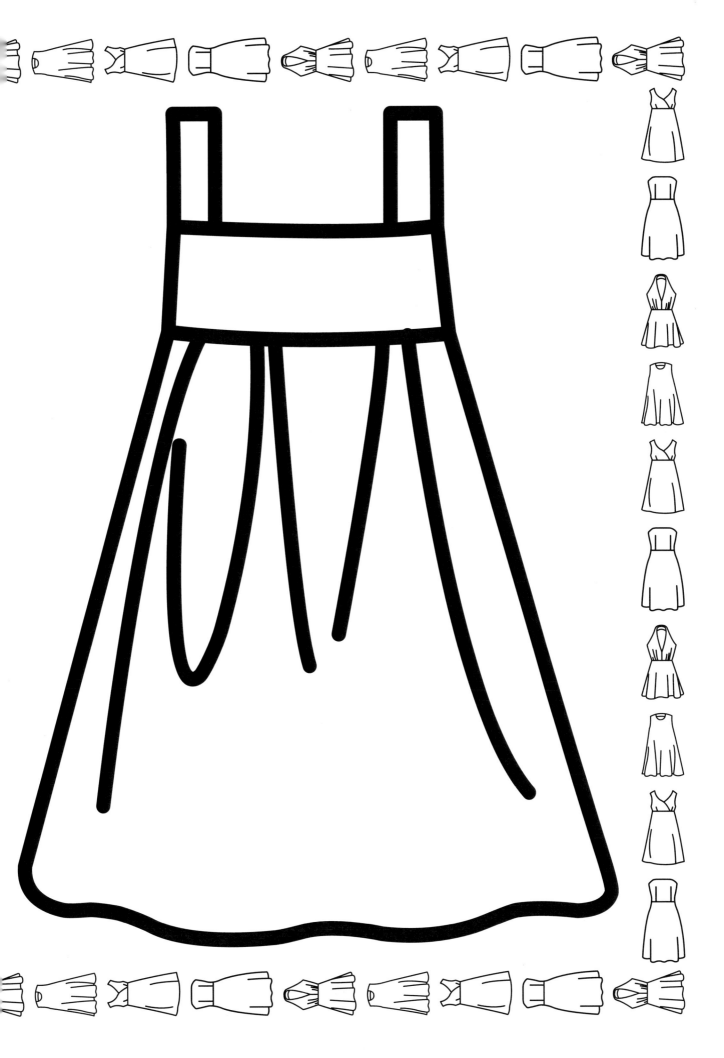

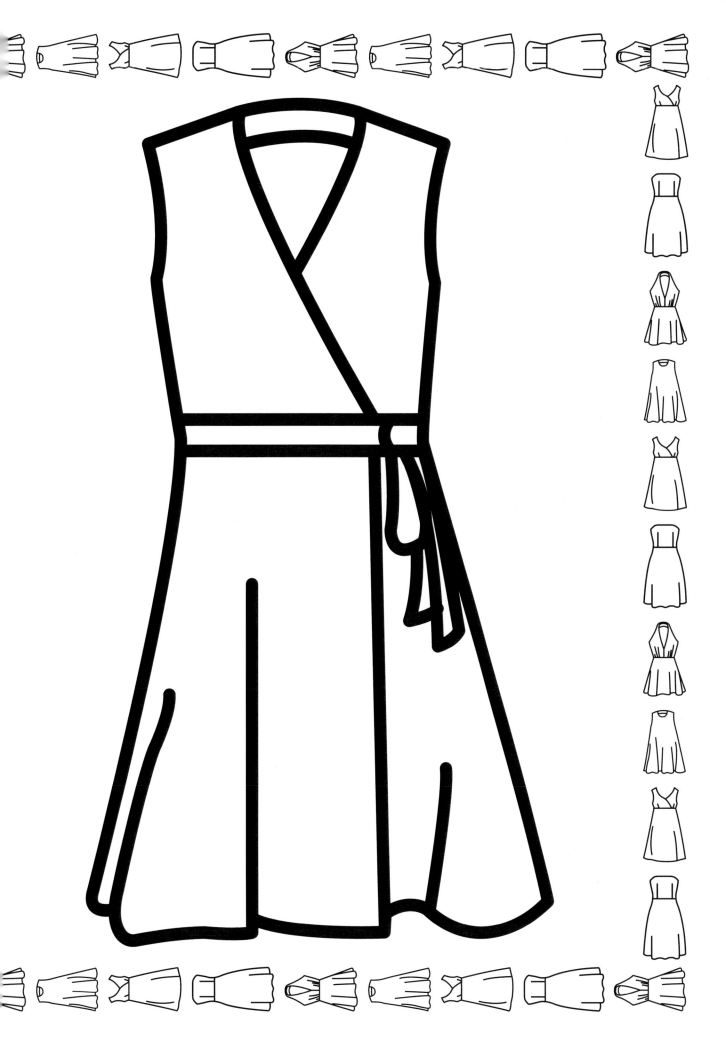

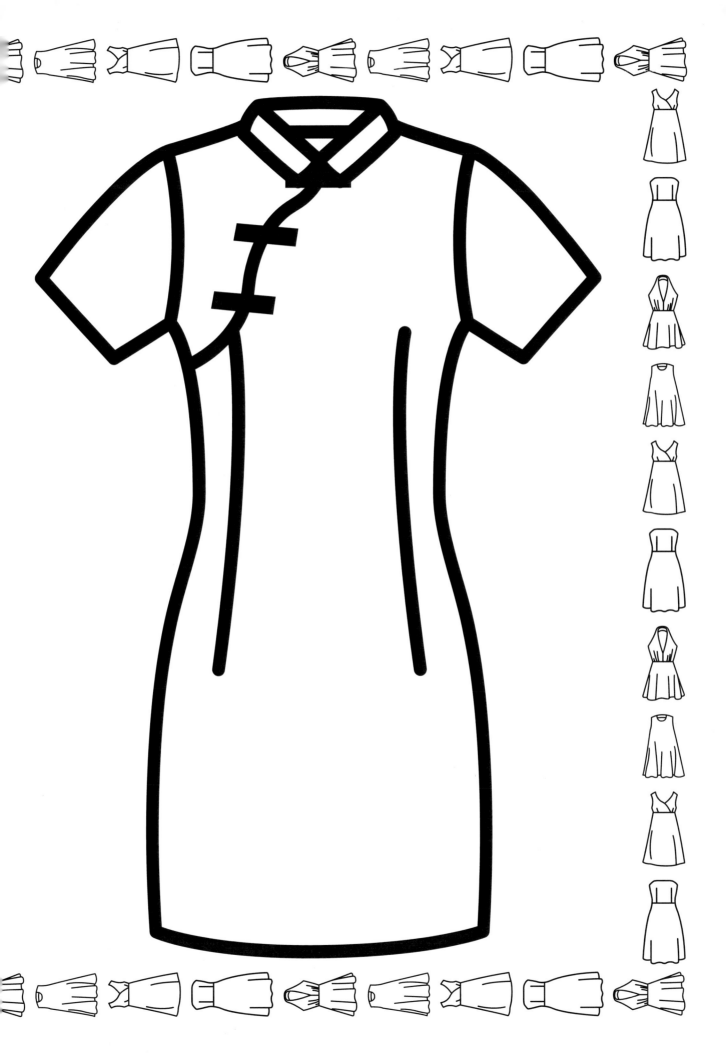

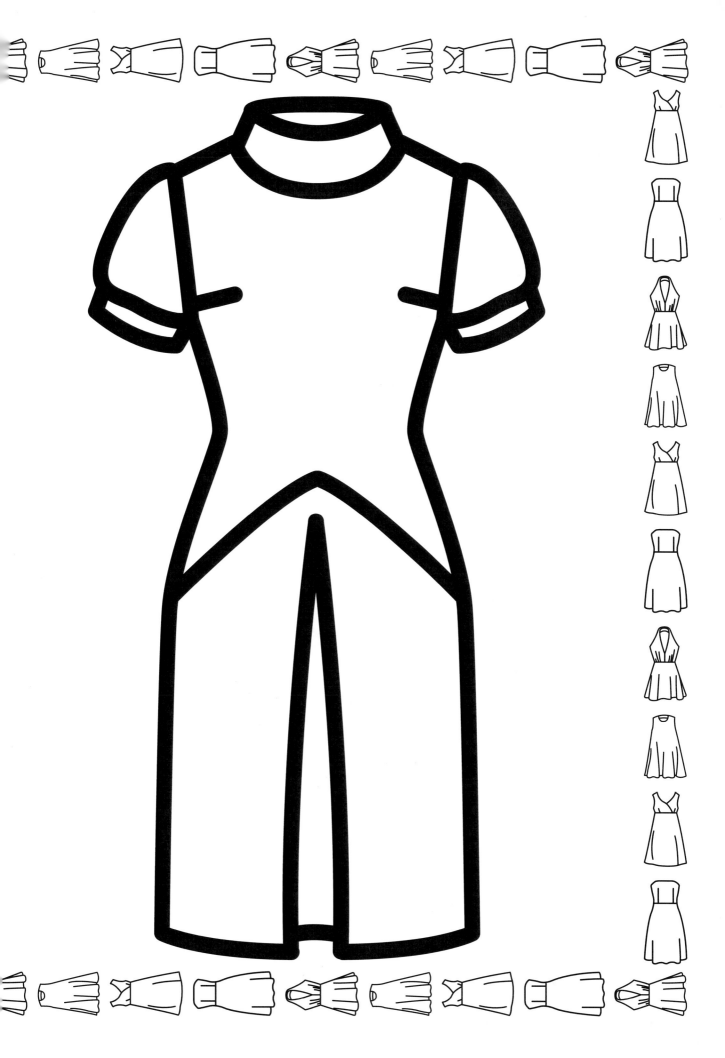

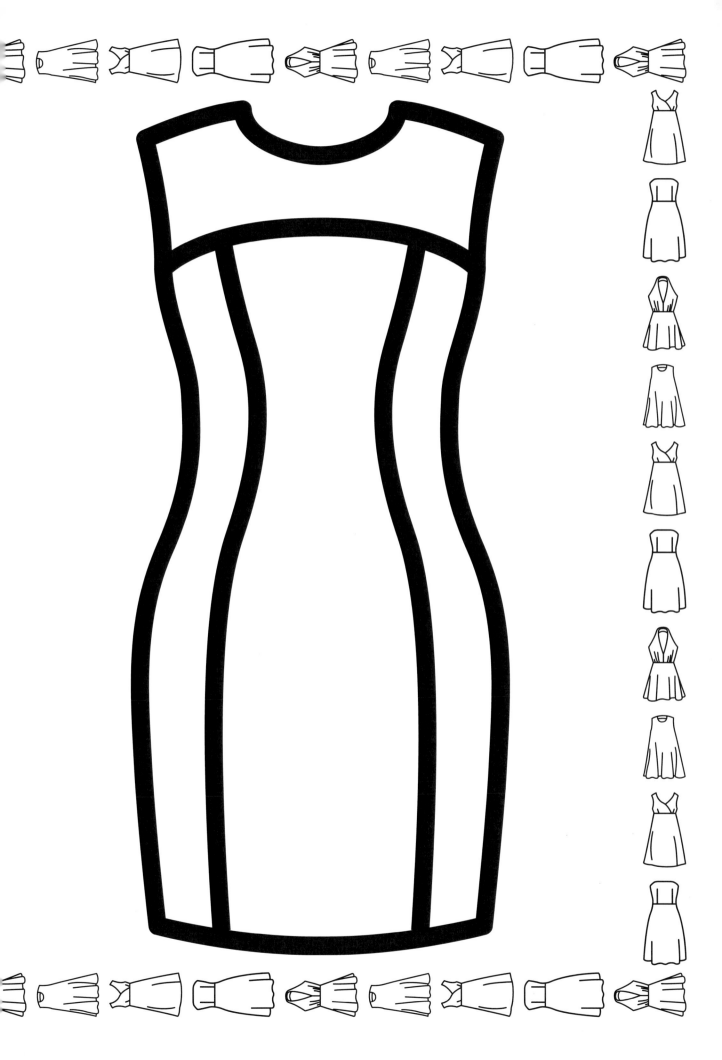

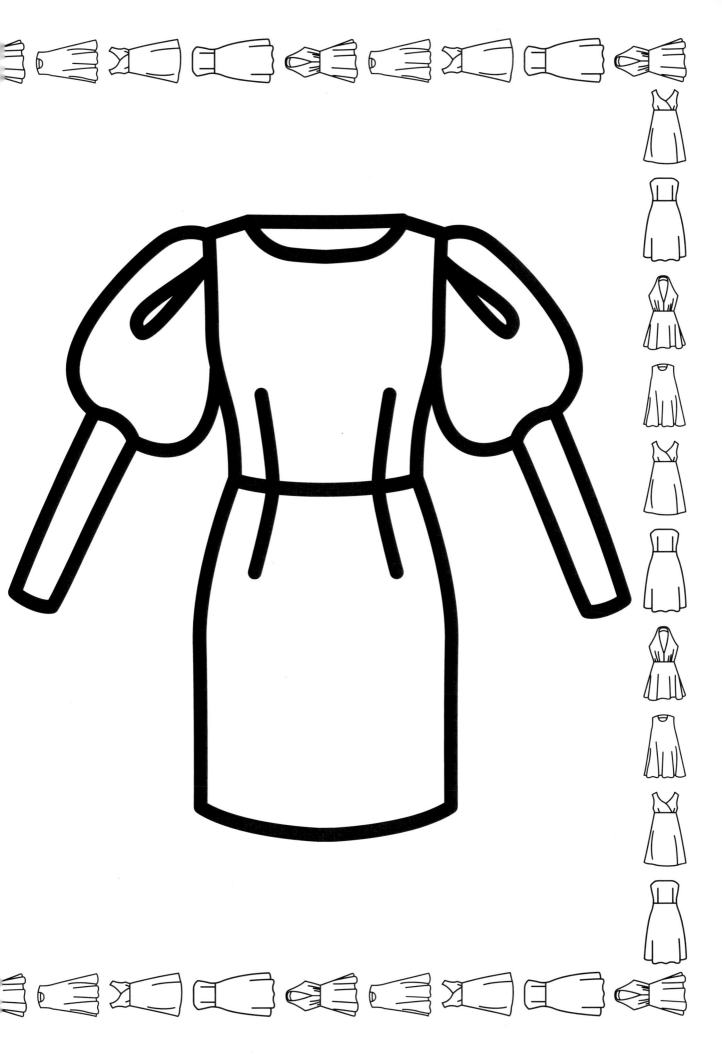

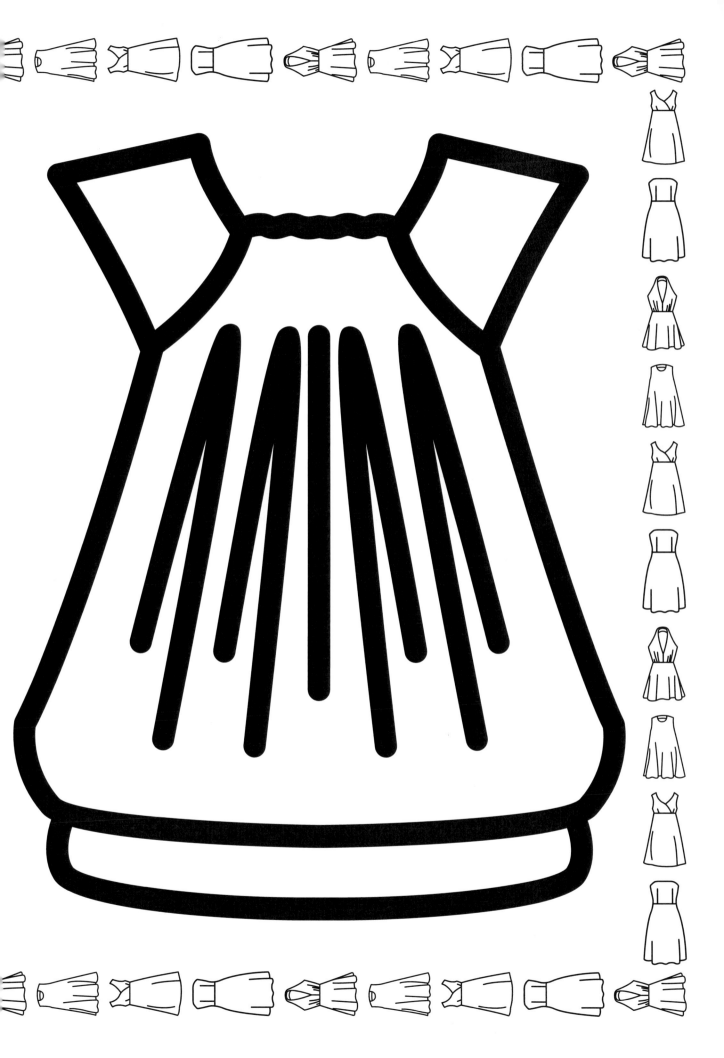

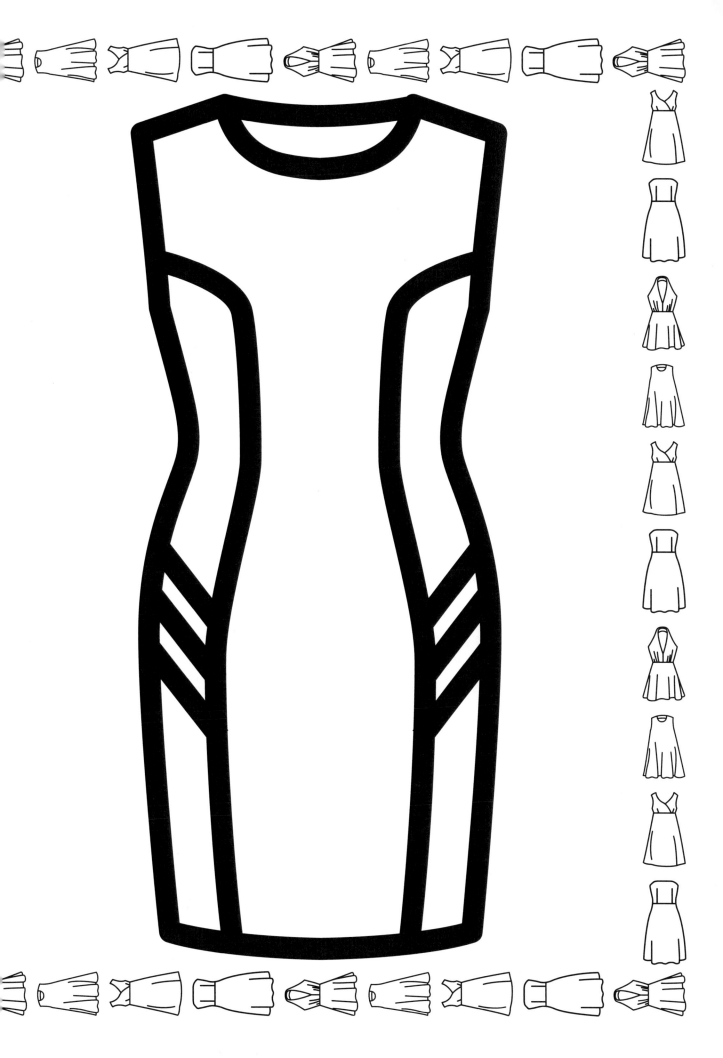

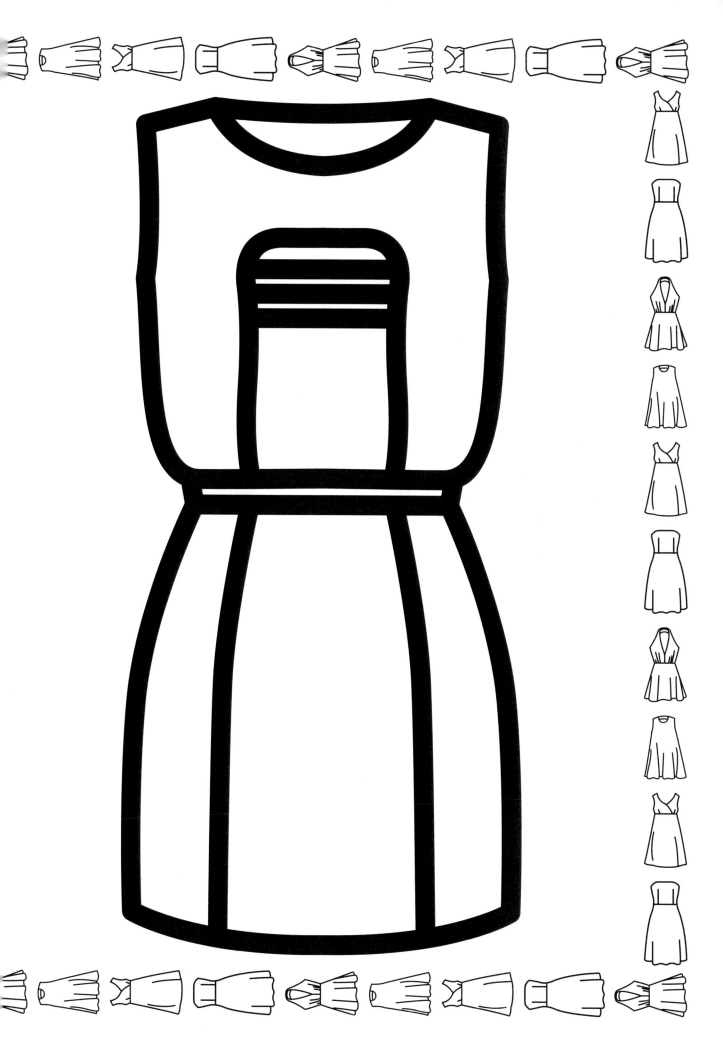

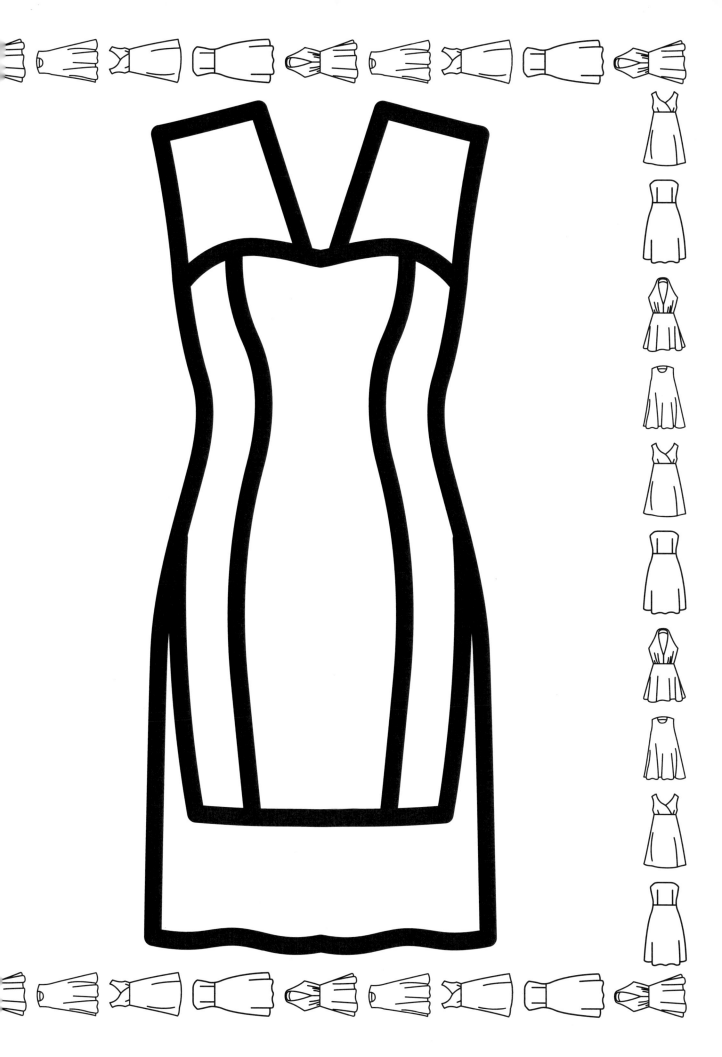

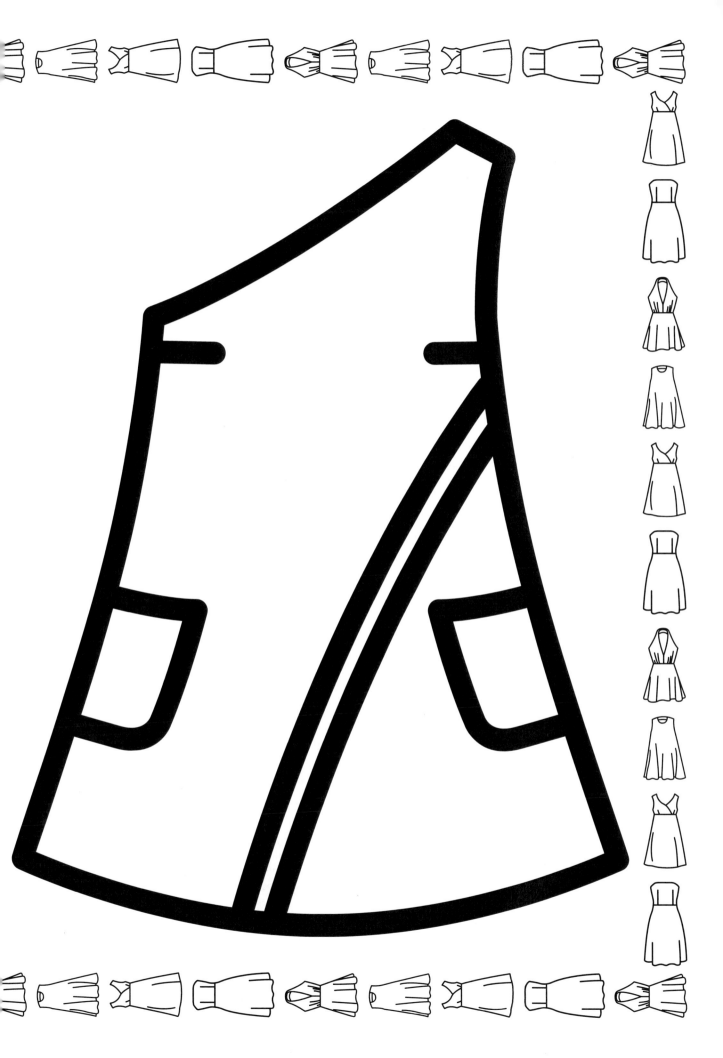

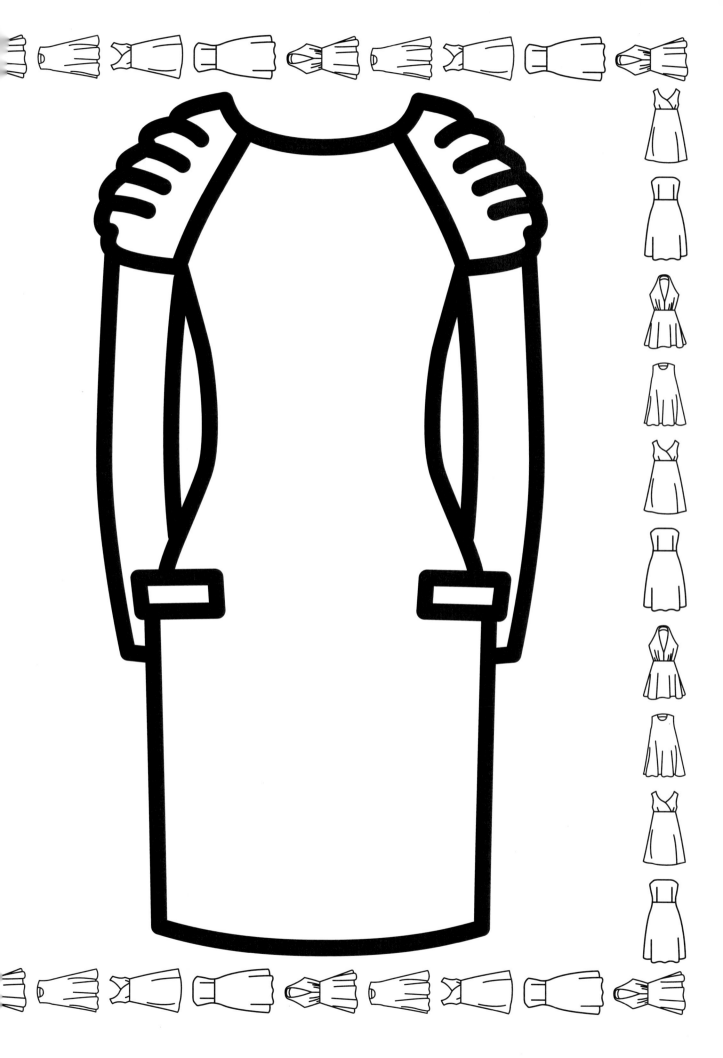

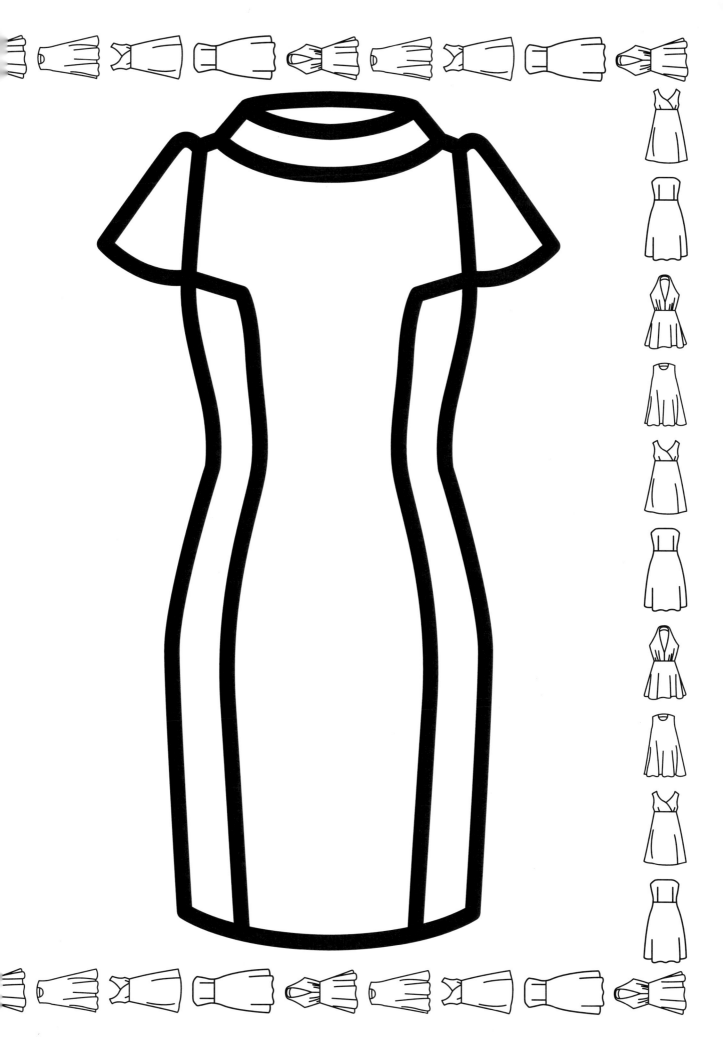

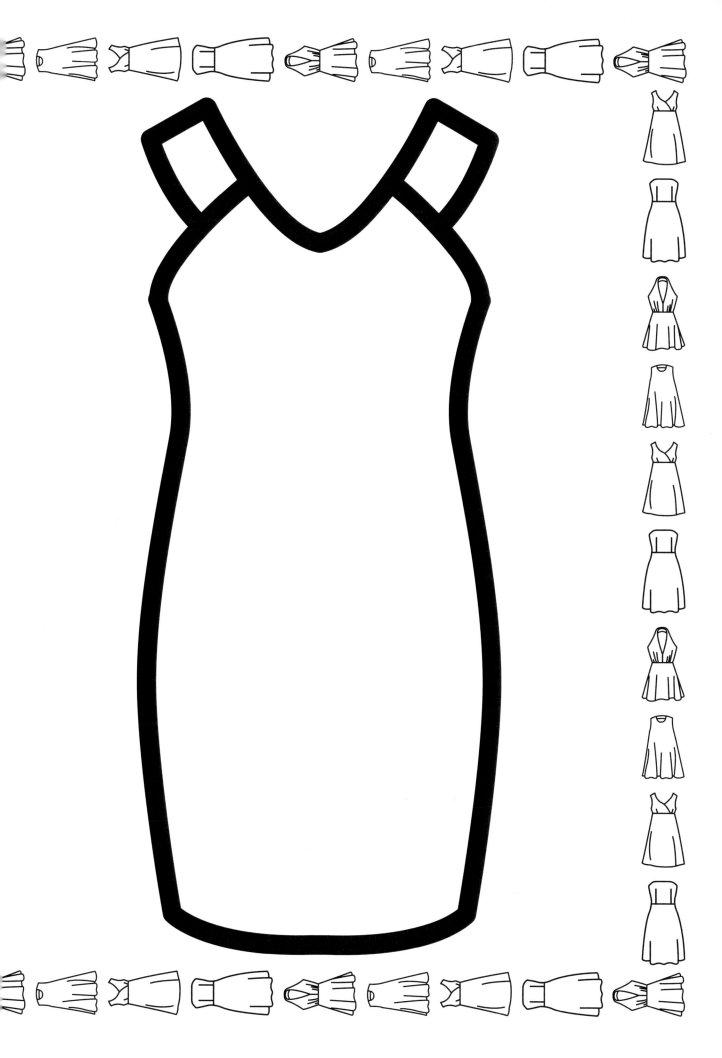

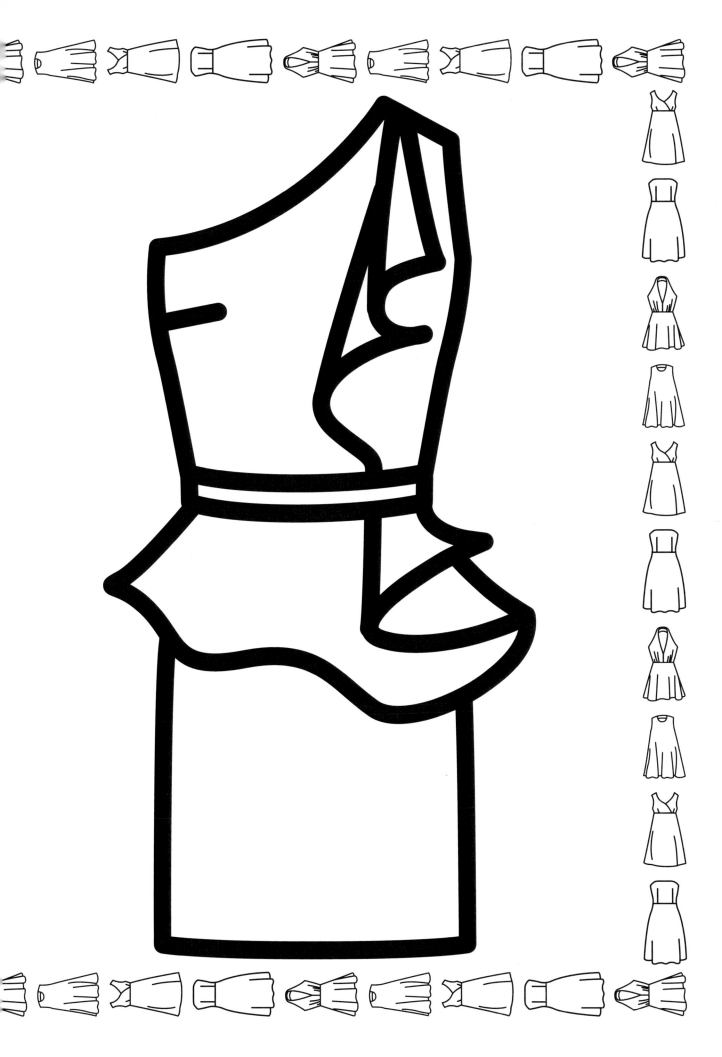

Made in United States
North Haven, CT
02 May 2023

36165630R00065